Want to get rid of your emetophobia?

Then read this practical guide and discover the proven natural ways to reverse your emetophobia for good.

Inside you'll learn...

* The safest and most natural ways to treat emetophobia.

* How to heal your emetophobia without drugs or surgery.

* How to get rid of emetophobia and start living your life again.

* How to banish emetophobia with simple home remedies.

* The most effective emetophobia treatments that doctors don't want you to know.

...and MUCH MORE!

So download this book and start to live your emetophobia-free life once and for all!

Those who suffer from emetophobia fear vomiting as well as being near someone who vomits.

In

the most severe cases, these people avoid eating out, socializing and attending parties or meetings for fear of having to vomit.

Many times it is a type of disorder that is combined with anorexia, since often those who suffer from emetophobia stop eating voluntarily.

People who suffer the phobia of vomiting are often affected their quality of life, because the fear of vomiting is constant and the feelings of discomfort to generate a panic attack when they are convinced that effectively vomit.

Emetophobes are so afraid of vomiting that they almost do not vomit and are able to endure nausea and at the same time become very rigorous and obsessive with food: they avoid certain ingredients because they think they can cause them intoxication, or certain foods because they relate them to an episode of vomiting in childhood.

Emetophobia is a psychological condition categorized within specific anxiety disorders. Like the rest of specific phobias, it is distinguished because the person suffering from it experiences a deep fear towards an object, person or specific situation.

In the specific case of emetophobia, this exacerbated fear comes before any stimulus related to vomiting. Although anyone can manifest feelings of aversion to him, in emetophobia the person experiences a deep sense of fear, which is also irrational, uncontrollable and remains over time.

The situations that can cause this response of anxiety in the person range from the act of vomiting, as well as seeing others vomit, such as the sensation of nausea that precedes the vomit or the vomit itself.

The causes of a phobia of vomiting

But what can this irrational fear of vomiting cause? As with all phobias, one of the most frequent causes is due to conditioning of a traumatic experience.

A gastroenteritis in childhood that was recorded, see your mother vomit from a pregnancy or the discomfort of a family member for chemotherapy, for example, are cases that have generated emetophobia.

I Got Rid of My EMETOPHOBIA After Years of Trying Every Drug and Medication!

--> Here's EXACTLY What I Did...

The fear of vomiting can also arise as a consequence of an anxiety disorder and can be cause and consequence of a disorder such as anorexia. In any case, whatever the origin, you must seek treatment as soon as possible.

Heal your digestive system

For this there are many therapies and treatments, from a change in your diet, colon cleansing, treatment with teas (infusions), certain juices, constancy in your diet, eliminate soft drinks, medical treatments ... etcetera.

The important thing is that you focus on your stomach and heal it, not medicate it and absorb the symptoms but actually heal it.

In the meantime, you can help yourself to a chamomile or lemon balm tea before eating, and then take a Tums pill or a glass of water with baking soda. As I say, are remedies that help you to lessen the sensations, but not to heal the causes ok?

What I do think is very important is that you focus on eating healthy and do not let more than 4 hours pass between meals.

ACONITUM is the medicine of people who live in a permanent state of maximum alert. They are agitated, nervous, impatient people. They want to prevent everything, to know everything to be prepared and face any adversity. They live as if they were permanently in mortal danger. It is the great medicine of acute panic attacks.

GREEN TEA AGAINST CELLULITE

Green tea (Camellia sinensis) is an excellent resource against cellulite.

It has a diuretic, antioxidant and lipid-lowering effect. Accelerates the combustion of calories and favors the metabolism of fats.

Drink green tea in infusion, as a diuretic. Another possibility is to use it in ointment, gel or anti cellulite cream.

HORSE TAIL TO DEPRIVE

With the retention of liquids and cellulite accounts with diuretic and depurative plants.

One of the most effective is the horsetail (Equisetum arvense). It is also remineralizing.

Use the sterile stems to prepare an infusion. Take two cups a day.

Alternatively you can use liquid extract or capsules.

Relaxation: The tension of the body and the muscles must be alleviated, maintaining the posture and the balance in the legs.

I Got Rid of My EMETOPHOBIA After Years of Trying Every Drug and Medication!

--> Here's EXACTLY What I Did...

Good humor: If what worries is that other people notice, you can try to tell a joke or release a comment that makes them see that the situation is known to release the anguish of knowing what others think.

Dismiss the situation: You should not give importance to something that really does not have it and less if others do not pay attention to it. The more you focus on the blush, the more it will appear.

Avoid situations that make you blush: For this you have to detect the moments or circumstances that cause the coloring.

Fermented foods

Do you like sauerkraut? All the better, she can help you take care of your health ... as long as you get rid of bacon and sausages.

Fermented food par excellence, the cabbage as it is prepared for this Alsatian recipe is full of benefits. This old process like the world helps us to digest well. Fermentation at room temperature boosts the content of probiotics, friends of the microbiota. It also boosts vitamins, essential amino acids, and produces nutrient enzymes and antioxidants.

Eating fermented foods also facilitates the assimilation of minerals, carbohydrates and proteins. If sauerkraut does not tell you anything, there are many others: kefir (a drink made with milk or fermented fruit juice), miso (wheat), kombucha (a sweet drink made from fermented tea), pickles or just yoghurt.

Peppermint essential oil Peppermint is one of the best essential oils to relieve the symptoms of diarrhea. Because it is both a painkiller and an anti-inflammatory.

Menthol, one of the active ingredients of peppermint essential oil, acts as an antispasmodic by blocking the calcium channels of the intestine. This can reduce intestinal cramps, as well as pain in the digestive system.